The Aborigines of Minnesota and their
Migrations

The Aborigines of Minnesota and their Migrations

(History of USA)

By Newton H. Winchell
with the contribution of John W. Willis

History and Civilization Collection

LM Publishers

The State of Minnesota is bounded on the South by Iowa, on the West by South and North Dakota — the Red River (commonly called the Red River of the North) separating it from the latter state — on the North by the Canadian provinces of Manitoba and Ontario.

The population of Minnesota at the first Federal census (1860) after its admission into the Union was 172,023, and by the succeeding Federal enumerations it was: (1870), 439,706; (1880), 780,773; (1890), 1,301,826, excluding Indians (10,096); (1900), 1,751,394; (1910) 2,075,708. For example, in 1900, of the total population, 932,490, or 53.2%, were males, and 818,904, or 46.8%, females; 1,246,076 were native-born; 505,318, or 28.9%, were foreign-born, and 1,312,019 were of foreign parentage (i.e. having either one or both parents foreign-born). Of the 14,358 coloured inhabitants, 4959 were negroes and 9182 Indians, 8457 of whom lived on reservations. The urban population (i.e. inhabitants of cities of 8000 or over) was 26.8% of the total population, as compared with 28.2% in 1890. By the state census of 1905 the population of the principal cities was as follows: Minneapolis, 261,954; St Paul, 197,023; Duluth, 64,942; Winona, 20,334; Stillwater, 12,435; and Mankato, 10,996; by the same census four other cities, all in the mining region in the north-east, had passed the 5000 limit, viz. Hibbing, 6566; Cloquet, 6117; Virginia, 5056; and Eveleth, 5332.

(Encyclopedia Britannica, 1911)

The Prehistoric Aborigines of Minnesota and their Migrations

It would have been considered an act of great temerity twenty-five or thirty years ago to enter upon an investigation of the Indians of Minnesota in prehistoric time. But, thanks to the rapid progress that has been made in aboriginal research in North America, chiefly under the guidance of the late J. W. Powell and his associates in the Bureau of Ethnology at Washington, it is now necessary only to apply to Minnesota some of the great truths that have been established as to the Indians at large, and to designate under those principles what Indian stocks and tribes have inhabited the state in some of the centuries that preceded the advent of the whites.

In order to clear the field at the outset by the removal of any obstacles that we may have inherited from earlier conceptions of the aborigines, it will be well to repeat some of the important results that have been reached within recent years, *viz*.:

1. The origin of the ancestors of the Indians was so remote that nothing yet discovered indicates its date or the source from which they came.

2. There are between fifty and sixty Indian stock languages, some of which are as distantly related as the languages of the various Aryan nations, but most of

which are as distinct as the English from the Semitic.

3. This shows that the aborigines, if they came at all to America, must have come from a great many directions, or that their coming was so remote that they must have developed these differences amongst themselves by long periods of isolated residence in North America.

4. The Indian stock languages cannot be connected, at least have not been connected as yet, with any convincing bond of relationship, with either European or Asiatic languages. The Eskimo are here not included, as that stock ranges from Greenland through North America into Siberia.

5. The aborigines, therefore, are indigenous to the soil of America in the

same sense that the Mongolian and Caucasian are indigenous in the lands of the Eastern continent.

6. The "moundbuilders," that fabulous race of Squier and Davis, were the ancestors of some of the Indian tribes of history. What those tribes were is gradually being unraveled.

7. The greatest number of the aboriginal language stocks were located along the Pacific coast, say in California, and along the Atlantic and Gulf coasts in the southeast; the interior of the continent being occupied thinly by only three or four stock tongues, these being Athapascan, Shoshonean, Algonquian and Siouan. The Kiowa, who also were in this central area, are thought by some to be an independent stock, but by others

related to the Comanches, and hence may, for our present purpose, be classed with the Comanches in the Shoshonean family. The Pawnee, or Caddoan, family was feebly represented in the interior of the continent aside from their main habitat at the gulf coast and in Texas; but the Iroquois shared with the other widespread families in the possession of the interior. These, however, appear to have linguistic alliances with the Cherokees and more distantly with the Siouan stock. Hence again, for the purpose of the present discussion, the Iroquois may be considered with the Siouan family.

Of these four great family stocks it will be the purpose of this paper to deal mainly with the last two mentioned, *i. e.,* the Algonquian and the Siouan.

POWELL'S MAP
OF
ABORIGINAL LINGUISTIC
STOCKS.
FROM THE SEVENTH ANNUAL REPORT
OF THE
BUREAU OF ETHNOLOGY
1885-86

In the Algonquian family are embraced the following tribes, as stated by J. W. Powell, as well as several other small tribes that dominated the north Atlantic coast; the arrangement here is that of D. G. Brinton in the previsional order of their linguistic affinities, the oldest and perhaps the parent tongue, the Kilistino, heading the list:

Cree (Kilistino)
Old Algonkin
Montagnais
    Ojibwa
    Ottawa
    Pottawotomi
    Miami
    Illinois
    Pea
    Piankishaw
    Kaskaskia
    Menominee
    Sac
    Fox
    Kikapoo
      Micmac

Etchemin

Abnaki

    Delaware

    Shawnee

    Mohecan

    Nanticoke

    Gros Ventres (of the Plains)

    Sheyenne

To these may be added the Arapahoe, associates of the Sheyenne in Wyoming, not mentioned by Brinton. These show, according to Krœber, certain characteristics that mark them as differing from the other Algonquians, both in speech and in tribal organization. There is no history or tradition of their origin.

They have no clans nor totemic divisions, whereas these are marked features of the most of the Algonquian stock. Certain more elemental characteristics of their dialect, and the certainty of their having long preceded the Sheyenne in their present habitats, seem to warrant the assumption that they are more primitive than even the Kilistino.

The area formerly occupied by the Algonquian family was more extensive than that of any other linguistic stock of North America, their territory reaching from Labrador to the Rocky Mountains, and from Churchill River of Hudson Bay as far south at least as Pamlico Sound of North Carolina. (Powell.)

The Dakotan, or Siouan, family comprised the following Indian nations, arranged approximately in order of apparent derivation:

Biloxi
Tutelo
Waccon
Catawba
    Huron Iroquois?
    Cherokee?
        Winnebago
        Omaha
        Osage
        Issati
        Mandan
        Missouri
            Dakota
            Iowa
            Ottoe
            Hidatsa (and Crows)

having numerous subtribes, *viz.*, Santee, Sisseton, Wahpeton, Yankton, Yanktonai, Teton, Blackfeet, Minneconjou, Ogalala, Ponka, Assiniboin, Akansea, Kansa and others.

The position above assigned to the Cherokee and Iroquois is conjectural, but is based on the statements of some authorities. Mr. Horatio Hale has sufficiently established the connection between the tongues of the Cherokee and the Iroquois, and Mr. Mooney has shown the relation between the Cherokee and the primitive tribes of the tongue in South Carolina. It may be that the alliance of the Iroquois with the Dakotan stock is so feeble that the two should be considered as separate stocks. But, for reasons that will appear, the Cherokee (Tselaki), the ancient Alligewi, seem to have had an ancestry which was cognate with that of the Dakota. It will be shown that they both moved from their pristine seat on the Atlantic coast in the Carolinas, where some archaic remnants of both tongues still continued in early American history.

The country occupied by the great Dakota stock, aside from the small tribes that remained near the Atlantic, was, in general, the "interior continental basin" so far as it lay west of the Mississippi River and east of the Rocky Mountains, with a broad tongue that extended into Canada so as to take in some of the waters that reach Hudson Bay, west of Lake Winnipeg.

It covered the Missouri Valley except in its utmost upper reaches in the region of the Yellowstone Park, which belonged to the Shoshonean stock, and excepting also the valley of the Platte. It extended eastward in a narrow tongue, across the Mississippi, through southern Wisconsin to Lake Michigan, an anomalous geographic exception, the important significance of which will be referred to later. As to Minnesota, it was divided between the Algonquian and the Dakota stocks, the larger part being in possession of the Dakota.

The Kilistino, an Algonquian tribe, were in the north and northeast, in the wooded region north of Lake Superior. Their dominion included the boundary waters not farther west than Kainy Lake, but continued unbroken to Hudson Bay.

A few other general considerations ought to be stated at this point in order to prepare for the discussion of the topic in hand. These are:

1. During the prevalence of the last ice-epoch the state of Minnesota was covered with ice, and all previous inhabitants, whether fauna or flora, were

driven southward to more congenial climes.

2. This condition ended between seven and eight thousand years ago. It is not necessary here to rehearse the investigations on which that result is based.

3. Between the ice-fields and the habitable portions of the continent lying to the south was a belt of country, the width of which varied according to the longitude and according to the topography, which was uninhabitable by reason of the severity of the climate. This uninhabitable belt may be compared to a belt in northeastern and northern Canada at the present time which is uninhabitable for the same reason. It was wider, however, than the

northern Canadian belt, and less ameliorated along the banks of the rivers. Their waters drained from the northern ice fields, whereas the Canadian rivers carry waters from southern and more temperate latitudes. But like the Canadian belt it was wider toward the west. The ice-margin and the accompanying severity of climate crossed the country from southeast to northwest. The prehistoric isothermals, same as the present, passed northwest-wardly.

4. Hence the habitable portions of the United States, until seven or eight thousand years ago when the ice began its retreat, were along the Atlantic seaboard south of New Jersey, a belt along the coast of the Gulf of Mexico, a

large interior area without ascertainable limits, and the Pacific coast west of the Sierra Nevada.

5. So far as Minnesota is concerned, and the same is true of much of the northern United States, it seems to be necessary, therefore, to confine all investigation of aboriginal migration to an antiquity not greater than seven or eight thousand years.

6. For Minnesota it is necessary to make a still further restriction, for it was the ice-margin itself that retired seven or eight thousand years ago from the vicinity of the falls of St. Anthony. It required, maybe, two thousand years more for the passage over the state of that uninhabitable belt already mentioned.

7. The people along the gulf coast and on the ocean shores would not have been quick to follow up the retiring cold of a glacial winter. They would not readily leave the warm lowlands, where food was abundant, to penetrate the wastes of a country that was still swept by cold winds and whose wide-spreading waters were chilled by the dissolution of the northern ice.

8. The occurrence, however, of an opportunity for migration was equivalent to the creation of an impulse, and after a time the southern tribes moved into the regenerated new country.

It is the purpose of this paper to give a glimpse of some of the movements of this migration, and to show how it affected Minnesota. The time within which these migrations occurred, for reasons already stated, cannot therefore exceed five or six thousand years.

It will be reasonable to assume that wherever the chance for hopeful migration first presented itself there the first movement took place. Some weaker tribe was expelled by war, or, the people being crowded, some tribe sought more room and better quarters to expand in. This change must have begun in the southwest, perhaps no further south than Utah or Colorado, or perhaps some tribe of Mexico began the great migration.

The same impulse toward northward migration was felt all along the gulf coast and on the Atlantic seaboard. Sometimes whole tribes abandoned their ancient seats and sometimes only a discontented portion of a tribe parted from their kindred. There must have been many conflicts and counter migrations and movements in all directions; but those who started first probably continued to move in the van as they were again pressed by those in the rear.

When there came finally a condition comparatively fixed, it must be allowed that the tribes had settled where their environment was best suited to their needs, subject, of course, to the dominance of more powerful tribes.

It may be reasonably accepted that on attaining a condition of comparative quiet, the geographical situation of the linguistic stocks was approximately as represented on the linguistic map of Powell, barring, of course, such later changes of habitat as can be shown to have taken place either within historic time or by consistent application of tradition. A general sketch of the Powell linguistic map has already been given.

It is now necessary to examine it a little more closely and to note some of the more remarkable features. It is a most notable fact that the southern parts of the United States are thickly dotted over with small areas that denote the locations of numerous distinct aboriginal stocks, while the broad interior is occupied by a few widely spread stocks that were, as is known, thinly dispersed along the river courses and ranged in pursuit of game or of their enemies occasionally over the plains.

The Athabascan stock, now occupying the interior of Alaska and of northern Canada, may be presumed to have been the first, or among the first, to leave their pristine seats. But they must have left a considerable number of their friends at home, since they still subsist in a large tract in eastern Arizona, western New Mexico and south- western Texas, under the names of Apache and Navajo, with their subdivisions.

The Shoshonean family may not have moved far from their pristine home, at least seem not to have entirely abandoned it, since the Shoshonean area still lies contiguous to the Pacific coast in southern California. They apparently simply improved the opportunity of expansion, and latterly perhaps dispossessed some weaker tribes. Still, it is quite possible that the Shoshonean people were powerful and spread over a wide interior area from which they have never departed even during the prevalence of the glacial climates of the north.

The two great Indian families, however, in which we are most interested are the Algonquian and the Siouan. Let us notice the contrasts in their distribution. The Algonquian spreads over the north-eastern part of the United States and Canada, with a small root lingering adjoining the Shoshonean in Colorado, but has no representative on the southeast Atlantic coast. It is true that according to the map the Algonquian stock extends as far south on the Atlantic seaboard as North Carolina, but this southward expansion there is of later date and can be excluded from the discussion. Indeed, the whole Delaware confederacy, covering the Algonquian areas in New Jersey, New York, and some portions of New England as well as all of that in the stales of Kentucky, West Virginia, Ohio, Indiana and the most of Illinois, can likewise be excluded, since, as will appear, their acquisition of those areas is of comparatively recent date.

It appears, therefore, if the Algonquian stock was governed in post-glacial time by the forces which have been mentioned, that that people started from the southwestern country, spread over the interior plains, and preempted the timbered regions of Canada and the northern United States. It hence follows that the northern part of Minnesota, Wisconsin and Michigan, and the most of New England were the first settled habitats, in the United States, of the Algonquian people. Prior to the Dakotan incursion, the Algonquian probably controlled areas farther south, especially in Minnesota, while the mainly uninhabited interior, i. e., the plains of the Missouri and of the upper Mississippi, were the fields over which for a long period of time all the surrounding nations sent war parties and hunters, but did not venture to make permanent settlements.

Now compare with this the distribution of the Siouan stock. It has two small areas on the Atlantic seaboard contiguous to similar areas of the Iroquois, but its main area is west of the Mississippi, embracing the wide plains over which roamed the buffalo.

These areas are separated by the states of West Virginia, Kentucky, Ohio, Indiana, Illinois and Michigan, where now reside the Algonquian, or at least where they were found by the Europeans when they made acquaintance with the region. Guided by the same principles, we may infer reasonably that, on the amelioration of the glacial climate, the

Siouan family, residing wholly on the southeastern Atlantic seaboard, migrated toward the north and west, crossing the mountains that bound them in, and sought the plains on the west. With the vicissitudes of war and the lapse of thousands of years, those who remained on the east side of the Alleghany Mountains were permanently separated from those who migrated, and the western tribes expanded rapidly over the western plains of the Missouri, becoming powerful and a scourge to their neighbors, "the Iroquois of the West," as they have been termed not inaptly.

We can infer, therefore, that these two stocks, the Algonquian and the Siouan, moving, one from the southwest and the other from the southeast toward the

Mississippi Valley, early came into collision, and that in the main the Mississippi River at first constituted the boundary line separating their domains. This early hostility became a hereditary war, and on the side of the Siouan stock the Iroquois also participated. I do not know of any record, and of but one tradition, of war between the Iroquois stock and the Siouan stock west of the Alleghanies, but both these stocks maintained bitter and hereditary war against the Algonquian.

The prehistoric Siouan people were neighbors in the Carolinas of the prehistoric Iroquois, and the two people more or less allied in language and having similar customs and the same opportunities for northward migration probably moved about simultaneously, both tribes crossing the mountains into the country where the waters flowed in the western direction, the Iroquois to the north of the Sioux.

It is a remarkable fact that, with the exception of the earthworks of the gulf coast, these two stocks are the only ones that have been found to have had a general custom of constructing earth mounds and embankments.

These common resemblances, regardless of any linguistic affinity, are sufficient to point to an early common origin. If the Algonquian stock in any of its tribes is found to have constructed mounds, such as those characteristic of the Ohio mound-builders, it seems to have been only exceptional or sporadic, or may be attributed to adoption from their neighbors belonging either to the Iroquois or the Siouan stock.

I know that Dr. Thomas has shown the great probability that the Shawnees, an Algonquian tribe, were the authors of certain mounds in western Tennessee and contiguous territory farther southeast, and specially of those that cover the characteristic stone-box graves. Admitting that, it is still true that the Shawnees have not been shown to have been mound builders in a wide sense, and that, carrying the habit of subsurface burial with them when they left their kindred and migrated into southern Illinois and western Tennessee, they might easily have adopted the custom of their mound-building new neighbors and covered their box graves with earth mounds. But, without admitting at present that the Shawnees constructed the mounds that cover the stone-box graves, it seems to be reasonable to refer those mounds to the predecessors of the Shawnees, *viz*. : the Osage and perhaps the Omaha, who belong to the Dakotan stock, and who have a tradition, which is confirmed by other traditions, that they once lived east of the Mississippi in that very region. With this understanding, it is, I repeat, a remarkable fact that, aside from the

Muskogean earth-works of the gulf coast, which have distinctive characters, only the Dakotan and Iroquois stocks can be shown either by history or tradition to have been characteristic mound-builders.

It is due to the research of the late J. V. Brower that the Dakota tribes of Minnesota have been proved to belong to the so-called mound-builder dynasty. But the mound-builder domain was, par excellence, in the Ohio Valley and southward into Kentucky, Tennessee and northern Georgia and eastward into West Virginia. There is also a remarkable series of effigy mounds in central and southern Wisconsin which extended across the Mississippi into Minnesota and Iowa. With slight exceptions the typical mound-builder area was occupied, as shown by Powell's map, at the coming of the whites, by non-mound-building people ; while the great body of the mound-builders, represented by the Siouan stock, were on the west side of the Mississippi, in a region which had been passed by, or ignored, by the early migrating stocks.

As between a prairie and a forested country it is plain that the forested area would be chosen first by the aborigines. Aside from the shelter afforded by the timber, the forests yield food more easily captured, as well as material for his habitation and for his implements of war and the household; while the annual devastation by fire rendered the prairie not only uninhabitable, but actually dangerous. It is certain, therefore, that the occupancy of the prairies has been, in general, the latest step in the establishment of the dominion of the aboriginal tribes.

In other words, it is only a late migration which has brought the Siouan tribes into the plains of the Missouri and of the upper Mississippi, and with this fact agrees all the evidence that can be found that bears on it, whether from a study of the people themselves, of the mounds, or of their traditions.

It will be anticipated, from what has been said thus far, that the original mound-builder dynasty in the Ohio Valley was destroyed by an incursion of hostile people belonging to the Algonquian stock. It will be the burden of the rest of this paper to establish that great prehistoric event, and to show what effect it had on Minnesota.

Dr. Cyrus Thomas is to be accredited with the most thorough investigation of the aboriginal earthworks of the country.

Under the direction of the Bureau of Ethnology he has established some important generalizations and has traced out some of the movements of the tribes that were concerned in the war which resulted in the expulsion of the original mound-builders from Ohio and the contiguous regions. Suffice it to say here that he considers that the evidence shows a movement, at least an extension, of the earliest mound-builders from the region of eastern Iowa, southeastern Minnesota, and southwestern Wisconsin, across Illinois and Indiana into Ohio.

He shows that these people were driven out toward the east and southeast. He traces this retreat, which may have required several hundred years for its completion, with the most patient and convincing research, and arrives at the conclusion that when the whites came upon the scene the defeated and expelled people were known as Cherokee, living in western North Carolina and eastern Tennessee, and were still building mounds.

The last statement is abundantly verified, even by historic documents. De Soto met them in his trip across the cis-Mississippi region, and his chroniclers describe the mounds which they saw.

Some of the mounds built by the Cherokee in their new home contain articles of European manufacture.

But this line of persistent aggression from the northwest to the southeast, resulting in the expulsion of the Cherokee from the upper part of the Ohio Valley, was not the whole of the great war, though it is the only part that has been established by evidence like that adduced by Dr. Thomas. It can hardly be questioned that such an incursion would have had a disastrous effect on the mound-builders of the whole Ohio Valley, and that they were all driven out at the same time and by the same hostile force.

It is necessary now to rely on tradition, and on the preliminary considerations already presented, to show what became of the rest of the moundbuilders of the Ohio dynasty. It is apropos, however, to remark that the whole of the mounctybuilding people could not have escaped by the route traced out by Thomas up the valley of the Kanawha River. By far the larger part of them had a habitat further south and further west, and the most probable line of retreat for them was down the Ohio Valley.

There are many traditions that relate to the migrations of the native tribes within the United States. I will call your attention to but two of them. These relate to the great movements that are here discussed, but they are confirmed by several others that supply contributory details, and when taken all together their force amounts almost to as great a body of evidence as if the events were a matter of history.

These two traditions have been accepted by all archeologists as trustworthy testimony, as far as the Indians could communicate a history of past events. The only differences of opinion that have appeared pertain to the interpretation and application of the traditions themselves.

One of these two traditions recounts the hostile incursion of the Lenni-Lenape, an Algonquian tribe or group of tribes, into the region west of the Alleghany Mountains, their conflict with the "Tselaki," a word which has been corrupted into Cherokee, and with the Allegewi, a word which is perpetuated in the term Alleghany, and their final settlement, under the name Delaware, in the eastern part of Pennsylvania and in New Jersey, together with some further migrations toward the east. The other relates to the migration of some of the Siouan tribes down the Ohio River and their going "up stream" and "down stream" on the Mississippi on reaching the mouth of the Ohio. I do not know that any one has called in question the essential parts of this tradition.

John Heckewelder, a Moravian missionary with the Delaware or Lenni-Lenape in Pennsylvania, gave the first printed account of the hostile incursion of the Lenni-Lenape against the Ohio mound builders. It is published in Vol. XII. of the *memoirs of the Historical Society of Pennsylvania*, in 1818. He took it from the relation of the intelligent Indians. With some abbreviation it is as follows:

"The Lenni-Lenape (according to traditions handed down to them by their ancestors) resided many hundred years ago in a very distant country in the western part of the American continent." For some reason they determined on migrating to the eastward, and accordingly set out together in a body.

After a very long journey, and with many long stops on the way, they at length arrived on the "Namaesi-sipu," which by Mr. Heckewelder is translated "Mississippi, or River of Fish" when they fell in with the Mengwe, who had likewise emigrated from a distant country, and had struck upon this river somewhat higher up. [The Mengwe were the Iroquois.] "Their object was the same with that of the Delawares : they were proceeding on to the east-ward until they should find a country that pleased them. The spies which the Lenape had sent forward for the purpose of reconnoitering had long before their arrival discovered that the country east of the Mississippi was inhabited by a very powerful nation, who had many large towns built on the great rivers flowing through their land." These people called themselves Tallegewi or Allegewi. [According to later research this is the aboriginal rendering of the name "Tselaki " which De Soto gives to the Cherokee when he encountered them at a much later date farther south.]

Many wonderful things are told of this famous people. They are said to have been remarkably tall and stout, and there is a tradition that there were giants among them, people of much larger size than the tallest of the Lenape. It is related that they had built for themselves regular fortifications or entrenchments, whence they would sally out, but were generally repulsed. I have seen many of the fortifications said to have been built by them.

When the Lenape arrived on the banks of the Mississippi, they sent a message to the Allegewi to request permission to settle themselves in their neighborhood. This was refused them, but they obtained leave to pass through the country and seek a settlement farther to the eastward. They accordingly began to cross the Namaesi-sipu, when the Allegewi, seeing that their numbers were so very great, and in fact consisted of many thousands, made a furious attack on those who had crossed, threatening them all with destruction if they dared to persist in coming over to their side of the river. Fired at the treachery of these people and the great loss of men they had sustained, and besides not being prepared for a conflict, the Lenape consulted on what was to be done, whether to retreat in the best manner they could, or try their strength and let the enemy see that they were not cowards, but men, and too highminded to suffer themselves to be driven off before they had made trial of their strength and were convinced that the enemy was too powerful for them. The Mengwe, who had hitherto been satisfied with being spectators from a distance, offered to join them on condition that after conquering the country they should be entitled to share it with them. Their proposal was accepted, and the resolution was taken by the two nations to conquer or die.

Having thus united their forces, the Lenape and the Mengwe declared war against the Allegewi, and great battles were fought in which many warriors fell on both sides. The enemy fortified their larger towns, and erected fortifications, especially on large rivers and near lakes, where they were successively attacked and sometimes stormed by the allies. An engagement took place in which hundreds fell, who were afterward buried in holes, or laid together in heaps, and covered with earth. No quarter was given, so that the Allegewi at last finding that their destruction was inevitable if they persisted in their obstinacy, abandoned the country to their conquerors, and fled down the Mississippi River, whence they never returned. [Mr. Heckewelder gives some further details of the war, the result of which was that the Mengwe, or Iroquois, chose the country round the Great Lakes and the St. Lawrence River, and the Lenape settled farther south. After a time the Lenape moved farther east, and even to the sea.]

They say, however, that the whole of their nation did not reach this country; that many remained behind in order to aid and assist that great body of their people which had not crossed the Namaesi-sipu, but had retreated into the interior of the country on the other side on being informed of the reception which those who had crossed had met with, and probably thinking that they had all been killed by the enemy.

The tradition continues further, but is not essential to this inquiry except so far as it shows that the Lenape finally spread themselves into the eastern states, establishing new tribes, and into Virginia and Maryland, and states that these younger offshoots recognized their relationship by calling the Lenape their grandfathers, this proving a confirmation of the recentness of the southern Algonquian tribes.

Several important conclusions can be drawn from this tradition, should it be accepted as mainly based on fact. First of all it should, however, be remarked that the well-known Iroquois were never on the Mississippi river in any such war. Either some other river must be understood, or it must be presumed that the alliance with the Mengwe was an event of the later part of the war, and that in the relation it was not sufficiently indicated that the Lenape waged alone a long war of aggression against the Allegewi and drove them from a large part of their domain before the Iroquois tendered their services.

The latter alternative is the more probable, since the Huron-Iroquois have only been known as an eastern nation, and since the legend would not so many times mention the Mississippi by name unless there was a grounded conviction in the mind of the narrator, which seemed not likely to be misunderstood, that the Mississippi was crossed by the Lenape.

We may reasonably infer from this tradition, in the light of what we know from a study of the mounds and their characteristic distribution :

1. That the Lenape struck the then mound-builders in southeastern Minnesota and northeastern Iowa, in the region of the effigy mounds, these earthworks being admitted by all to be older than the great mass of the small tumuli of the Mississippi Valley.

2. There was a period of interruption in the war during which the aggressors

rested and dwelt peacefully in the land which they had won.

3. On the resumption of the war not all of the Lenape participated, but some remained on the banks of the Mississippi. These may have become known later as the Kaskaskia, Kikapoo, Illinois, Miami, and further south, the Shawnee. It is distinctly stated that a large body remained, some "beyond the Mississippi" and others "where they left them on this side of the river" in the words of the missionary.

Mr. G. E. Squier (1848) later examined this tradition. He fell into the possession of a series of original manuscripts, "through the hands of the executors of the lamented Nicollet" among which was one by Professor C. S.

Rafmesque, which was entitled the "Walum Olum" a record preserved on painted sticks, translated by Rafmesque from the original symbols and the Algonquian words written along with them by some interpreter who understood both.

Omitting those portions relating to the creation of the earth, to the deluge and the running off of the waters which show the effects of contact with the European missionaries, I will briefly mention the views of Mr. Squier and the points of coincidence or divergence from the rendition of Heckewelder. Mr. Squier says :

The details of the migrations here recounted, particularly so far as they relate to the passage of the Mississippi and the subsequent contest with the Tallegwi or Allegwi, and the final expulsion of the latter, coincide generally with those given by various authors, and well known to have existed among the Delawares.

According to the Rafmesque rendition, as given by Squier, there were two great wars. The first was after a migration from the north to the south, attended by a contest with a people denominated Snakes, who were driven toward the east, and the Lenape remained for a time in their land, and multiplied and spread toward the south to a beautiful land which is also called "big-fir" land. In consequence of drouth they move again south into the buffalo land. Here they dwell for some time, when finally their chief leads them toward the rising sun and they arrive at the "Messissipee" or the Great River, the

Mississippi, when they stop ; but they soon descry the Tallegwi and make war upon them.

This war continues through the lives of several chiefs, but ends by the expulsion of the Tallegwi who were driven southward, the victors taking possession of the land where they resided and flourished under a long succession of chiefs. Here they built towns and planted corn, and here, after the expulsion of the Allegewi, is the first mention of the Iroquois, and instead of being their allies they are enemies. They are called Talamatan and Mengwe.

Then commences, apparently, a repetition of the same narration in different words and more in detail, a characteristic feature of many ancient records and legends. In this account, the Lenape departed from a northland, where it was cold and froze and stormed, and they went south to possess milder lands abounding in game. They hunted in all directions and came to the Snake land, whose inhabitants fled in great fear.

The pursuers passed over a hard, stony and frozen " sea" and came to the land of fir trees, which they called "Shinaki."

After the lapse of an indefinite time, during which they remained in the land of firs and came into hostile contact with several of the surrounding people, among whom are Chiconapi, Makatopi, Akonapi and Assinapi, they passed " over a hollow mountain " and found food in the plains of the buffalo land, along a yellow river, where they built towns and raised corn, and remained for a long time, under a number of different chiefs.

Becoming dissatisfied, they "longed for the rich east-land," and on moving in that direction they came into conflict with the Tallegewi. "The Talamatan and the Nitilowan all go united " (to the war) ; and fell upon and slew great numbers of the Tallegewi. Sometimes they were repulsed by the Tallegewi, but finally all their towns were captured and they fled to the south, and the Talamatan (Hurons?) settled north of the lakes, the Lenape on the south side, i.e., in the land of the Tallegewi.

The rest of the chronicle pertains to later movements in Pennsylvania and New Jersey and their early dealings with the English.

According to both these renditions, all those events preceding the crossing of the Mississippi may have taken place, and probably did, in the region extending from the Hudson Bay southward to the northern boundary line of Iowa, or some miles farther south. The Snake land is problematical, but seems to have been in Canada. The crossing of the frozen water may have been the crossing of the Bainy Lake, or some of the contiguous waters. Shinaki, the land of firs, is the pine-clad region of northern Minnesota. The Assinapi could not have been the Dakota

Assiniboins, but may have been some Indians living in the same rocky region.

The Buffalo land may have been the southern part of Minnesota and northern Iowa. The "Yellow" River, where they raised corn, may have been that which by the early French was called "La Jaune riviere" now known as Vermilion River, uniting with the Mississippi a little below Hastings, and it is probable that the Tallegewi, as before, were the effigy-builders of the Wisconsin-Minnesota-Iowa region of the old mound-builders. Their movements through the country east of the Mississippi, according to one of these renditions, was marked by the friendship and later by the hostility of the Talamatan.

It remains to notice one more interpretation of this tradition, that of the late Dr. D. G. Brinton. On a previous page has been given the arrangement which Dr. Brinton presents of the tribes of the Algonquian, having the Cree dialect, which is that characteristic of the region of northern Minnesota and thence northward to Hudson Bay, at the head of the list. Dr. Brinton remarks of this:

The dialects of all these were related and evidently at some distant day had been derived from the same primitive tongue. Which of them had preserved the ancient forms most closely, it may be premature to decide positively, but the tendency of modern studies has been to assign that place to the Cree, the northernmost of all.

Accepting this indication for what it may be worth, it certainly points to the Cree, or Kilistino, as being not only more nearly connected geographically with the primitive habitat of the Algonquian, but also as representing their ancestors' tongue more nearly than any other dialect of the Algonquian stock. This will allow the post-glacial migration of that stock from the southwest, as has been supposed, perhaps from Colorado and Wyoming, where they seem still to have a representative in the Arapahoe.

The Cheyenne who are now associated with the Arapahoe are later comers, having joined the Arapahoe from the northeast within the historic period. On this supposition, the dialect of the Arapahoe would prove, on close comparison, to be more archaic than all other Algonquian dialects, holding for that stock the same position as that held for the Siouan stock by the Catawba dialect in South Carolina, and the late researches of Kroeber bear out this presumption.

As to the tradition itself, it should be premised that Dr. Brinton, along with Horatio Hale, had a belief that the American aborigines had all migrated from the Atlantic coast westward, having reached America from Europe, derived perhaps from some obscure people in the northern part of Spain. Mr. Hale, who seems to be the chief supporter of this view, in referring to migrations of the Indians quotes only historic movements, which certainly have been largely westward, due probably to the encroachments of the whites since the Columbian discovery.

It is simply a geographical and historical accident that we are more familiar with the migrations of the eastern Indians than we are with the western. Under the influence of this preconceived idea, which, according to Mr. W. M. Beauchamp, was based on simply a linguistic " likeness " to one or more of the Indian tongues, Dr. Brinton has taken, it seems to me, great liberties with this tradition, insomuch that he has reversed the direction of the main movement, making it westward instead of eastward, thus making it conform to the direction of historic migrations, with which he seems to think it should be made to agree.

He supposes the Lenni-Lenape "at some remote period dwelt far to the northeast, on tidewater, probably Labrador.

They journeyed south and west till they reached a broad water full of islands and abounding in fish, perhaps the St. Lawrence about the Thousand Islands." This is quoted verbatim from Dr. Brinton. With similarly violent alterations from the legend, the Lenape are carried into Ohio and Indiana and thence back again to northern New York, having united with the Talamatan (Hurons) to drive out the Talega or Cherokees from the upper Ohio, which they only succeeded in doing finally in the historic period. These alterations from the sense of the tradition, as formerly understood, he claims to be warranted by the discovery of errors in the earlier translations.

The Snake people are relegated to myth, perhaps with correctness. He thinks the legend here relates a conflict between the Algonquian hero-god and the serpent of the waters, a myth which is found also among the Iroquois. After the conclusion of this conflict, the people found themselves in a cold northern country, whence they departed in search of warmer lands. Not recognizing the repetition in the legend of the same story, Dr. Brinton has the Snake war continue on through, and after, the settlement in Shinaki or the "land of spruce pines." Then comes the Lenap

'Allegewi war and the possession of the conquered country.

Neither time nor your patience would warrant me in entering upon a detailed consideration of the validity of the changes introduced by Dr. Brinton. I have carefully examined some of them that have some geographic relation to the country concerned, and will mention only that relating to the so-called "Yellow" River, where, according to the legend, the Lenape dwelt and raised corn "on a stoneless soil." Dr. Brinton considers this stream (Wissawanna) a small river in Indiana, a branch of the Kankakee, saying that on Hough's map of Indian names of Indiana that word has been corrupted to " Wethogan," and that the Minsi, one of the Lenape sub-tribes, were found there in 1721 by Charlevoix, and that they made their first migration from the east about 1690. This involves a historical anachronism, inasmuch as it makes an event occurring in 1690 to 1721 explain a doubtful point in a legend which is wholly confined to prehistoric time. If the Yellow River was first named in 1690-1721 it is not likely to have had that name when the Lenape were waging their war in prehistoric time before they had yet settled in New Jersey.

Again the region is said to have a "stoneless soil," which could hardly be affirmed of northern Indiana. But if the reference of the tradition to a "Yellow" River be not to the Missouri, as has been supposed by some, there is a Yellow River in Minnesota, if another is needed, *viz.*, that now called Vermilion River, entering the Mississippi below Hastings, which, indeed, has a stoneless soil. From there southward extends the " driftless region " on the east of the Mississippi, and in that vicinity are the first of the effigy mounds, i.e., in the Cannon Valley and in Goodhue and Wabasha counties and extending southward, while on the east side of the Mississippi is the central and most characteristic region of effigy mounds. It is not at all improbable that the migrating Lenape made a long halt in the valley of the Vermilion, contiguous to these mound-builders before they entered upon the great war.

This is the first of the great legends to which I called your attention. The second is that which brought the Dakota tribes into Minnesota, and it doubtless pertains to a time nearly cotemporary with that which refers to the Lenape. It comes to us from the other party to the great conflict, and it no doubt refers to the consequences of the Lenape invasion. This legend is found amongst several of the Dakota tribes, and even amongst the later Algonquian who returned westward to the Mississippi Valley.

I will not dwell on the details with those separate tribes, but simply mention the tribes with which it has been handed down from generation to generation, *viz.*, Osage, Omaha, Mandan, Kansa and

Akansea, and Ponca. These tribes concur in saying that they formerly dwelt in the Ohio and Wabash valleys, and that they moved down the Ohio Valley, where they were separated into two divisions at the mouth of the Ohio River, some of them going down the Mississippi and some of them up the same river. They repeated such segregation at the Missouri, where, as it appears from the preservation of the name, the Mantane divided into two parties, one of which became the Mandans and the other the Mantanton, the latter being one of the tribes of the Issanti at Mille Lac in 1701 when these tribes were enumerated by Le Sueur, at Fort L'Huillier. The name Issati or Isanti, is itself, apparently, another form of a name of the Siouan South Carolinan Santee, and sometimes, even now, it reverts to the original spelling. If so, they preserved their name during their long residence in the Ohio Valley as moundbuilders.

This tradition is linked in with some historic data in about the same manner that the Lenape migration is linked, and verified by some scant connection with historic events. With this migration the territory of Minnesota was almost wholly occupied by the Siouan stock, and that stock controlled it till the last incursion of the Ojibway from Lake Superior, when, with the great battle of Kathio, another culminating event of the hereditary war took place.

This brings us to recent time in Minnesota and it is not necessary to enter upon later tragic events.

There is still, however, one other point to which I wish to refer, viz., in coming to Minnesota those mound-builders who ascended the Mississippi above the mouth of the Wisconsin River returned to their former home. They may have recognized it as the scene of their first defeat by the Lenape, and probably some of them remained there and resumed the construction of mounds. It is admitted by all who have given attention to the subject that the effigy mounds are of a class distinct from and older than 'the tumuli that are scattered amongst them and which prevail in Minnesota and Dakota. The "Winnebago may have been effigy-builders when the Lenape crossed the Mississippi. If so, they must have fled northward from their enemies, instead of southward, and thus escaped the fate of their kindred. They perhaps remained in southern Wisconsin during the whole Lenap'Alligewi war, and so probably welcomed the fugitives on their return. This may account for that curious geographical extension of the Dakota stock on the east of the Mississippi in a narrow tongue reaching Lake Michigan; and it also accounts for the fact that linguistically the Winnebago dialect is one of the oldest of the Siouan stock found in the upper Mississippi region ; and further, that the Winnebago are called "grand-fathers" by the other tribes.

Thus it appears that the mound-builder dynasty was divided into two parts by a great national misfortune. The Ohio dynasty endured a long period of time. It was probably coeval with the effigy mound- building period or closely followed it. The Minnesota dynasty is comparatively recent, and was short, at the utmost not exceeding 500 years, and extended down to the incoming of the whites.

In conclusion, I can make the merest reference to another prehistoric migration affecting Minnesota, of later date than the preceding. It is well established by coherent and reliable tradition that the Hidatsa Indians, associates of the Mandans on the upper

Missouri, also called Minnitari, of the same stock as the Mandans, migrated from Minnesota across the prairie and settled with the Mandans.

We see then that the succession of dynasties in Minnesota is as follows :

1. Algonquian (small area in the southeast also held by the Ohio mound-builders).

2. Siouan, fugitives from Ohio (establishing the Minnesota dynasty of mound-builders).

3. Ojibwa (Algonquian) incursion from Lake Superior, dividing the state with the Siouan people.

4. Aryan civilization.

Brief History of Minnesota[1]

Before its explorations by white men, the Minnesota was inhabited by people of two great divisions of the American race. From the southern boundary of the state the land was inhabited by the Dakotas, while the shores of Lake Superior and the northern portion of the state were occupied by the Ojibways. Many places in Minnesota bear Indian names, and those derived from the respective languages of these two aboriginal nations show very clearly at the present time the areas which they respectively occupied.

The French came into contact, first with the Ojibways and the other kindred

---

[1] Based on the work of John W. Willis.

Indian nations of the Algonquin family, who in their language designated the Dakotas the Nadouessioux (Ojibway for "enemies"). The French soon abbreviated this long word into its final syllable, and called the Dakotas the *Sioux*, under which title they have been commonly known since the days of Marquette and Allouez.

The real history of Minnesota may be said to begin in 1680 with the visit to the Falls of St. Anthony and adjacent regions by Rev. Louis Hennepin and his companions, Accault and Augelle. During the same year Sieur Daniel Greyolson du Lhut explored the northern part of the state, and, in July, joined Father Hennepin at the lake now known as *Mille Lacs*. Late in the autumn du

Lhut and Hennepin departed from the land of the Dakotas and returned to eastern Canada. From the time of these explorations to the English conquest of Canada in 1760, France held sway over the Upper Mississippi region.

Practical measures were taken to secure the rights of France. A map of the year 1700 shows a fort on the west side of Lake Pepin. In 1695 a second post was established by Le Sueur on an island above the lake. Thus, in the beginning of the ei ghteenth century, what was officially termed "La Baye Department", consisting of a line of military and trading posts, was organized to command the waterways from Green Bay to the Falls of St. Anthony. Not until 1727, however, were systematic efforts made to establish permanent military garrisons north of the mouth of the Wisconsin River.

In the spring of 1685 Governor De La Barre of New France sent from Quebec to the west twenty men under the command of Nicholas Perrot to establish friendly alliances with the Dakotas. Proceeding to the Mississippi he established a post near the outlet of Lake Pepin, which was known as Fort Perrot. War having been declared in 1687 between the French and the Indians, Perrot and his followers left the Mississippi River and repaired to Mackinac. Early in 1689, however, he returned with a party of forty men to his post on Lake Pepin, and re-established trade with the Dakotas. On a map published in 1700 this fort is denominated Fort Bon Secours; three years later it was marked Fort Le Sueur, but it was in that year abandoned. In a much later map it is correctly called Fort Perrot.

In 1700, acting upon the recommendation of the Governor of Louisiana, Pierre Le Sueur, a native of Artois, France, came to the area now known as Minnesota with an intelligent ship carpenter named Penicaut and about twenty others, in search of copper which, according to earlier explorers, existed in the Sioux country. Le Sueur and his company spent the winter of that year in the neighbourhood of the great bend of the *Minisotah*, and there gathered a large quantity of green earth which was supposed to contain copper in the crude state. From the circumstance that this earth is sometimes described by Le Sueur and his contemporaries as "blue earth", that name has been given to the tributary of the Minnesota River at the mouth of which Le Sueur spent a winter and built a fort, and also to the country within which the site of the fort is situated. The Dakota word *Mahkahto* means blue or green earth, and that word, corrupted in the course of time to *Mankato*, is the name of the county seat of Blue Earth County.

A trading company, formed in Montreal to carry on traffic in furs with the Indians of the Baye Department, dispatched on 16 June, 1727, an expedition under René Boucher to the land of the Sioux. The expedition arrived at its destination on the shore of Lake Pepin on 17 September. Two Jesuit missionaries, Michel Guignas and Nicholas de Gonnor, accompanied Boucher and his small command. Before the end of October a small fort, called *Beauharnois* as a compliment to the Governor of New France, was built in the low lands opposite the towering cliff, which now bears the name of Maiden Rock.

A chapel was erected within the enclosure of Fort Beauharnois, and was dedicated to St. Michael the Archangel. This was the first Christian temple to cast its beneficent shadow upon the soil of Minnesota. The first ceremony of note in the new chapel was the celebration of the feast of St. Charles of which Father Guignas writes: "We did not forget that the fourth day of the month [November] was the saint's day of the general. Holy Mass was said for him in the morning, and we were well prepared to celebrate the event in the evening, but the slowness of the pyrotechnists and the variableness of the weather led to the postponement of the celebration to the fourteenth of the same month, when some very beautiful rockets were shot off, and the air was made to resound with a hundred shouts of 'Vive le Roy' and 'Vive Charles de Beauharnois' . . . . What contributed very much to the merry-making was the fright of some Indians. When these poor people saw fireworks in the air and the stars falling from the sky, the women and children fled, and the more courageous men cried out for mercy, and earnestly begged that we should stop the astonishing play of the terrible medicine."

It may be stated in explanation that, among all the American Indians, any phenomenon which exerted a powerful influence upon the physical and nervous system was designated by a term corresponding to the term medicine in other languages.

In a report made in October, 1728, by the Governor of Canada to the Government of France, Fort Beauharnois was said to be badly situated on account of freshets "and, therefore," as the report says, "this fort could be removed four or five arpents from the lake shore without prejudice to the views entertained in building it on its present site." The report declares that the interests of religion, of the service, and of the colony demand that the fort on the banks of Lake Pepin be permanently maintained. In S eptember, 1730, Fort Beauharnois was rebuilt on a plot of higher ground near the old establishment. Upon this lofty site, surrounded by some of the most beautiful scenery in America, now stands the Ursuline convent, Villa Maria. The convent chapel very properly bears the same name as its historic predecessor, St, Michael the Archangel. Sieur Linctot was made commandant of the new fort in July, 1731, and in 1735 was succeeded by St. Pierre. The Dakotas having shown a very hostile spirit, St. Pierre decided to abandon Fort

Beauharnois, and accordingly, on 17 May, 1737, the post was burned. In 1743, and again in 1746, representative chiefs of the Dakota nation made a journey to Quebec and presented to the Government of New France a petition for the re-establishment of the fort and for the restoration of trade relations. Their request was not granted until 1750, when Pierre Marin was commissioned to rebuild the little fortress. Fort Beauharnois was retained until the outbreak of the war between the English and the French, but it was never occupied after the surrender which followed the defeat of Montcalm in the famous battle of Quebec (1759).

About one-third of the state, compromising its north-eastern part to the east of the Mississippi was included in the territory surrendered by Great Britain under the treaty of 1783, at the end of the War of Independence. The greater portion (about two-thirds) of the territory embraced within the boundaries of Minnesota, however, was included in the Louisiana Purchase, ceded to the United States by France in 1803. In 1805, a grant of land nine miles square, at the confluence of the Mississippi and St. Peter (now Minnesota) Rivers, was obtained from the Sioux Indians. A military post was established on the grant in 1819, and in 1820 arrangements were made for the erection of a fort, which was completed in 1822 and named, at first Fort St. Anthony, but later Fort Snelling after the commanding officer. The grant has ever since been known as the Fort Snelling Reservation. In 1823 the first steam boat ascended the Mississippi as far as Fort Snelling, and annually thereafter one or two trips were made by steamboats to this isolated post for a number of years.

From the date of the English victory over the French to the establishment of Fort St. Anthony by the Government of the United States, conditions were unfavourable for the establishment of Catholic missions in the upper Mississippi country. However, some colonists from Switzerland, who possessed the true Faith and spoke the French language, having migrated from their original settlements near Fort Garry in Canada to a place seven or eight miles below the Falls of St. Anthony, Bishop

Mathias of Dubuque, whose diocese included the entire region now called Minnesota, visited Fort Snelling and the adjacent Swiss settlement in 1839, and in the following year sent a missionary to Minnesota, Father Lucien Galtier. The latter established himself upon the present site of the metropolitan city of St. Paul, and in the following year built a log chapel which he called by the name of the great Apostle of the Gentiles. The gradual increase of population about the chapel, the development of the community into a village, and finally into a large city under the name of St. Paul, constitute an important material monument to the missionary work of Father Galtier, and forever associate the name and fame of the capital city of

Minnesota with the glories of the Catholic Faith.

Minnesota was organized as a Federal territory by Act of Congress of 1849, and, on 11 May, 1858, its territorial existence terminated and it became a state…

www.ingramcontent.com/pod-product-compliance
Lightning Source LLC
Chambersburg PA
CBHW021207020426
42331CB00003B/237